For dear Henry,
My family and friends
Who have encouraged me so much.

Sometimes a word spoken or a scene captured drops a 'seed' into my mind and it may grow into a poem or a picture.
This combination of both has been gathered over many years and inspired by friends, travel and reflective moments.

1970
CHAMBERY
1970
·1992·
WYNDHAM
ESTATE
BIN
555
SHIRAZ
1945
L Prosser

The Cup.

Is your cup of life half empty? Is your cup half full?
Is there much that tries to push you? Other things that pull?
Step aside and now consider, Look at your life's cup,
Difficult it may seem, but, it's time to fill it up.

Now's the time to reconsider all you do and are,
Choose the things that motivate you, stretch and take you far.
Focus on your life's enrichment, treasure every day.
Each a gift to hold and value, not let slip away.

Make a framework for your values; have a simple plan.
Then build in your dreams and wishes, you know that you can.
Make a place for loving service, one for caring too,
Take time to appreciate all that life gives to you.

As you start to change your focus, look inside your heart.
So much treasure from your own life makes the perfect start.
Be determined, conscientious, as your plan builds up,
Rewards will come and you will have your overflowing cup.

At times of change in our lives, we need to refocus. This was one of those times.

Pink Golden Morning.

Dappling waters of grey, blue and purples,
Steel grey horizon that rises to blue,
Stillness and beauty, just the faint sound of lapping,
Of a vast, gentle ocean as the sun's breaking through.

Shadows and sunlight, the day is just dawning,
Ships of all sizes are crossing the bay,
O what a glorious 'pink, golden morning',
Never more wonderful start to the day.

'Peace', as the wind is just breezing and blowing,
'Peace', as the ocean is still as can be.
'Peace' as the sounds of the birds just awaking,
Giving a peace that sinks deep into me.

Shortly all life will start stirring and buzzing,
Noises and people will send out the warning,
Day has begun and life is for living,
This is the end of my 'pink, golden morning'.

The early morning scene overlooking the beach at Mojacar, Spain.

The Gateway.

In my minds eye I can see a gateway set in stone.
When I go through, which I often do,
I'm there with God alone.

It's a special place for me, I'm welcome every day.
Quiet and still, I take my fill,
And then go on my way.

What I love about this place is I can just be 'me'.
I don't pretend, I don't defend,
That's how it has to be.

Any pressures that I feel, from outside or within,
Are all laid down upon the ground
Before I enter in.

I know that when I contemplate;
take time to rest and pray,
My strivings cease, and I find peace,
That helps me through the day.

My friend described this picture of meditation to me whilst visiting in New Zealand. I love what it portrays, for her and others.

Song of the morning.

Beautiful chorus, chirping and calling;
The wonderful song of the early morning.
Not always seen, but you know they are there,
Almost like laughter, they sing without care.
The birds are awake and they herald the dawn,
Then sweetly and cheerfully welcome the morn.

One calls to another, the message is clear.
The answer returns from a partner quite near,
Their songs echo back and forth over the trees,
A real conversation that's carried on breeze.
As I sit and listen, its joy to my heart,
The early morn chorus, how every day starts.

For hours they sing on, not needing to rest,
Their joy rises up and cannot be suppressed.
No matter what weather, bright sun or sweet rain,
Their chorus repeats itself over again.
No nothing can stop the deep joy that they know,
They express it and put on a wonderful show.

And I have a deep joy that God gave to me;
It isn't dependent on what life can be.
It isn't affected by good or by bad,
Or whether I'm happy or whether I'm sad,
The deep joy of God is always enough,
And its there as my strength when the going gets tough.

Can I rise above problems and still sing His praise?
Let the joy of the Lord reign supreme in my days?
Can I be as constant as the early morn bird?
Will my joy be my strength? Will my praises be heard?
When I hear that sweet chorus, my heart has to say
I will join and worship at the start of each day.

Alone?

Sometimes I stand alone, and it might well have been my choice.
Sometimes I want to speak and I might be a lonely voice,
Sometimes I crave my solitude and in it I rejoice,
But I'm not lonely.

Sometimes the circumstances may exclude me from the band,
Some people be unfriendly, rather pushy or off hand,
I may feel somewhat small; not like the others who feel grand,
But never lonely.

And sometimes I feel confident and hold my head up high,
It's as though nothing can stop me and the limit is the sky,
I feel as if I've wings and that I'm learning how to fly,
And I can do it.

I know that what I want is to be true to what I feel,
And that includes true to my heart where God is very real.
Not carried by the throng who want my joy and peace to steal,
And I'll go through with it.

I know that I am standing in a place that has been proved.
My feet are on a rock that isn't easily moved,
A place where I am cared for and I know that I am loved.
Not on my own.

My dearest friends, so precious, and their company is great,
So many special times we spend and memories create,
So nice when kindred spirits find such joy as they relate,
I'm not alone.

Stag in Glen Cannich

L Prosser

Sydney.

Sydney Harbour, in all its splendour,
a picturesque place by the sea,
For a visitor it is so welcoming,
and a wonderful place to be.
The atmosphere- so charismatic,
so vibrant, friendly and kind,
So much going on, but we saunter along,
Relaxed in the joy that we find.

The Opera House stands in her glory,
her sails reaching up to the sky,
Her beauty unique and outstanding,
as the ferries and boats sail on by.
Activity pulses around you,
the young and the old quite content;
The musicians play, it's a wonderful way
To enjoy sunny days as they're meant.

There are cafes and bars on the quayside,
and a strong cosmopolitan air,
There are seats all around, if you need one,
to take time to stop and to stare,

Tower buildings provide a grand back-drop,
of hotels and the business world too,
But as you look out, there is never a doubt,
That the sea is the one calling you.

And out on the sea, what a vista!
The vast Harbour Bridge, steely grey
Looks down on the brilliant blue water
and lets all the ships pass her way.
There are yachts so tall and graceful,
and ferries and sleek streamline cats,
And the people all flock, to one of the docks,
To go travelling by this one or that.

If you take the time to be friendly,
greet people of each walk and climb,
They enrich the day you are spending,
and make it a memorable time.
Acquaintances can be so lovely,
not friendships – they take time to grow,
A chance meeting can mean so much fun in-between
The expected things that we know.

Majestic Green Mountains.

Majestic green mountains with folds down their backs,
Creating dark shadows of green and of black.
Some covered with timber, some bare to the sun,
Some bush-clad where natures' been given free run.

Majestic green mountains with folds on your backs,
I taste the adventure when I follow your tracks,
I see the pukekos by water and streams,
And I laze in the sand dunes and follow my dreams.

The ocean, so mighty, keeps pounding the shore,
Keeps pounding and pounding and pounding some more.
The sand always shifting, first low and then high,
And the sea keeps reflecting the shade of the sky.

Majestic green mountains your bush reigns supreme,
Prolific and varied your lush evergreen.
And my favourite, the Punga Fern stands proud and strong,
Its beautiful fronds and dark tendrils so long.

And sometimes, I wonder, how long will it be?
Till I come back again all this beauty to see?
For I've come to love it, and feel it's a part
Of something so special that's deep in my heart.
I know I can't keep it, it can't be my own,
But it is my own treasure, if only on loan.

Inspired by the Kapiti Coast in New Zealand. Here the bush clad mountains come down to the nature reserve, the sand dunes and then miles of spectacular beach and ocean breaking waves. Pukekos are intense blue wader birds.

Summer day in autumn.

A summer day in autumn, a rare and special treat.
The dusk and dawn so chilly, but the midday sun has heat.
You waken to bright sunshine, the sky is blue as blue.
Remaining birds are singing and there's such a heavy dew.

The spider's web is glistening, his prey he won't release,
And as you stand there listening, the air is filled with peace.
The cliff top walk is beckoning, so through the woods you go,
And then you are descending to the rocks and sea below.

It's steep, the track is winding, the woods and bushes clear,
The sight is just breathtaking, only sea and birds you hear.
Then sit a while, be watchful, let tensions drain away,
Enveloped in pure nature on this Autumn Summers' day.

When God made all this beauty, He made it just for me,
And if I can appreciate His love in all I see,
It helps me to feel close to Him, assures me He is there,
And helps me to remember I'm always in His care.

A glorious summer day in autumn, whilst here in Sark,
October 2005. Painted in the style of David Bellamy.

Winter.

Our lives have all the seasons
as we walk along with God.
We pass through spring and summer
as we take the path Christ trod.
We also know the harvest
and harsh winter comes in turn.
It's then we seek the Saviour,
and we wrestle and we yearn.

'Why, why are you far off Lord?'
are the words we often cry.
The heavens seem as brass,
it's just as though He's passed us by.
We reach out to embrace Him,
we wonder if He's gone.
Have we got the strength
of character and faith to travel on?

Our God has plans to train us,
make us strong in faith and deed.
To fill us with His spirit,
so in Him we can succeed
In overcoming problems
as our lives to Him we give,
Undeterred by circumstances
and the stress of life we live.

So, take us through the winter,
Lord, and bring us into spring,
Let's see new life emerging,
causing heart and voice to sing.
New growth, new strength, new beauty.
Let us stand for all to see,
What a mighty, faithful God
can do in such as you and me.

Painted in the style of Geoff Kersey

Prosser

My Friend.

I haven't heard from him for months and then my friend appears!
He creeps up on me suddenly, his presence undetected,
And often when he does arrive he hasn't been expected!
Announce himself? He does not, nor sends greetings or good cheer,
But silently creeps up on me, O yes, the snow is here!

How beautiful and dazzling on the mountain ridges high.
And resting on the trees until their colours are all gone.
And balancing on fence posts as the snow falls on and on.
Like crystals, no, like diamonds, that sparkle in the sky,
The landscape is transformed, in quiet, for the passer by.

Excited children grab their sledges running for the hills.
T heir laughter fills the air where once snow's peace had been.
They start their races down the slopes some running in between.
They roly poly in the snow their lungs the cold air fills,
A fun filled day is on its way, the snow, the thrills and spills.

And after we have marvelled at the beauty of the snow,
We seem to tire so quickly inconvenienced by weather.
We can't get out unless we dig. "Will this go on for ever?"
Our joy is overshadowed by the temperature so low,
And in the end our fickle hearts just want my friend to go!

A hard Winter in the Highlands, 2009/2010

The Thrush.

Honey gold, speckled chest, back – chocolate brown.
The song Thrush is busy, quite low to the ground.
I hear him each morning, his song rich and sweet,
I hear her crack snails for her young ones to eat.
She isn't too nervous, she doesn't mind me,
As I sit and I watch her, contentedly.

She runs and she hops from the bough to the ground,
Returning with whatever food she has found,
Then after some weeks, a young thrush comes through
And he hops around looking at what he can do.
He finds a nice meal of a snail he has smacked,
After just a wee practise, he's got the shell cracked.

For some time it's quiet, the birds must have flown,
Or ventured afar to a garden unknown.
Then one day, I see him, some food in his bill
And he cocks his head, winks and stands perfectly still.
"Oh you're quite safe", I say, as I slowly walk on,
And he stands his ground bravely and waits till I've gone.

I love all the thrushes and I hope they will stay,
I hope they won't travel and fly far away,
"If you stay I will feed you when the weather is cold,
We can strike up a friendship if you care to be bold
I'm new around here, but I think you are not,
So I hope that you stay in this beautiful spot."

Whilst living in Sark we had many thrushes living in the garden. July 2009

Here's to Returning.

We raised our glasses, it's time for a toast.
"Here's to returning" the words of our host.
"Yes, here's to returning" we chinked our reply,
And the seed of returning was in my minds' eye.

Returning back home from vacation is good.
Back to familiar things well understood.
But returning again to a home far away,
Brings both sadness and joy as approaches the day.

"Returning" conjures up many things.
The prospect of joy that reunion brings.
As we travel onwards to a different shore,
We'll look forward to visits we hope are in store.

Returning to family, recouping our joys,
Delighting in progress made by our boys.
Their own lives progressing, independent they stand,
But they'll love our returning, our being at hand.

Returning home again, back to our nest.
Establishing patterns that work for us best.
Supporting each other, hearts quiet and stilled,
But life overflowing, both rich and fulfilled.

How many times has my heart returned?
My spirit been hungry, my soul deeply yearned?
Just for the closeness of God by my side,
Morning and evening, each turn of the tide.

I raised my eyes and said "time once again",
Time for returning, not time to remain
Where I am in my walk, but time to move on,
To walk closer to God, and walk close to His son.

So I continue to practise anew
The presence of God as I journey through.
My path may take steps which are low or are high,
But the 'seed of returning' is in my minds' eye.

Written after 5 months away travelling in New Zealand and Australia

Autumn.

As autumn approaches,
The temperature changes,
It's time to celebrate harvest again.
My favourite season,
For so many reasons,
The beauty of nature will always remain.

The colours are changing,
Nature re-arranging,
Preparing to show off its beauty with pride.
The trees in their glory,
They all tell a story,
Which part I love best it is hard to decide.

The birds disappearing,
The golden leaves falling,
The landscape is changing so stark, bare and brown,
But the promise is there
And with God's endless care,
In the spring it will flourish; turn round.

It's the same in our lives,
If we rest or we strive,
He still watches over each step of our way.
And He helps us to grow,
To bear fruit and to know
That His strength is our strength for each day.

'Early snow over Loch Meiklie' The view from my home in Glen Urquhart

Quiet Evening Sunset.

Quiet evening sunset,
Colours all ablaze.
Peaceful, restful moments,
As I sit and gaze.
Silhouettes of pine trees
Frame the sinking sun,
Such amazing beauty,
When the day is done.

Quiet evening sunset,
Settling all round me,
As I sit and wonder
At everything I see.
Up above, an eagle
Soars through open sky.
Never let these moments
Ever pass me by.

Quiet evening sunset,
I must take my time
Always to enjoy your
Vista so sublime.
Always to implore you
'Rise and set some more',
So I can enjoy all
The sunsets in your store.

L Prosser

Lilies.

Consider the lilies of the field,
they do not work or strive,
They do not have to struggle,
to grow or stay alive.
They're there in all their beauty,
to see as we pass by,
We really can't compete with them
no matter how we try.

Consider the birds up in the air;
they don't build a store
Of food to keep for winter time
in case there is no more.
They soar and fly, they sing their song;
and take rest here and there,
Perhaps we should consider who
it is who has their care?

There must be a creator.
For all things that have grown, are
Far too great and wonderful
to have happened on their own,
And if that same Creator
is there to oversee,
If I trust Him; how much more will
He take care of you and me?